CAUGHT READING

Mir Tamim Ansary

PEARSON

CONTENTS

Reading is not just a tool for doing well in school. It is an important tool for living in the real world.

INTRODUCTION: GET CAUGHT READING IN THE REAL WORLD

Letter Groups

tion The letter group **tion** is an ending that you can add to some words. You know how this letter group sounds in the word **direction**. You will find the same letter group as an ending in one of your new words: **information**. See if you can read this word by breaking it into four parts: **information = in + for + ma + tion**. Can you read the word? Write it in the sentence below.

I would like some _____ about dogs.

Words to Know

	Look	Say	Picture	Write
almost al-most	☐	☐	☐	_____
article ar-ti-cle	☐	☐	☐	_____
Dana Da-na	☐	☐	☐	_____
fill	☐	☐	☐	_____
form	☐	☐	☐	_____
important im-por-tant	☐	☐	☐	_____
information in-for-ma-tion	☐	☐	☐	_____
list	☐	☐	☐	_____
paragraph par-a-graph	☐	☐	☐	_____
piece	☐	☐	☐	_____
sign	☐	☐	☐	_____
skill	☐	☐	☐	_____
sport	☐	☐	☐	_____
tool	☐	☐	☐	_____

Word Attack

+s   Add **s** to the words below to make the new words.

ad _____ article _____

form _____ sign _____

skill _____ sport _____

paragraph _____

+ing You can add **ing** to **shop** to make a new word. But write one more **p** after **shop** before you add **ing**. Write the new word in this sentence.

You can't go _____ if you have no money.

2=1 You know the words **news** and **paper**. Put them together to make one new word.

news + paper = _____

GET CAUGHT READING IN THE REAL WORLD

You are about to start the last book—**Caught Reading Level 7**. In the first six books, you learned about 1,000 words. You learned skills to help you read science, social studies, and literature.

Reading, however, is not just a tool for doing well in school. It is an important tool for living in the real world. You need to read in order to drive a car, look for a job, go shopping, rent a place to live, or fill out a form. You need it to get information from ads, read signs, and vote. You have to read a newspaper to find out what is going on in sports, politics, and the news as a whole. You have to read to follow directions—how to run a DVD player, learn a skill or a sport, fix a car—the list goes on and on. In fact, reading comes into almost every part of life today.

This book describes some of the forms of writing you may come across in the real world. You will learn how sentences are put together to build one main idea in a paragraph. You will learn how paragraphs are used to build one or more main ideas in an article. Some of the pieces in this book are articles about forms of writing. Others tell the story of two young people, Dan and Dana, who are just starting life on their own. You will see how Dan and Dana use information from ads, newspaper articles, and other forms of writing as they make their way in the world.

 Each time you see **MCR** it is time for a Memory Chip Review. Remember to practice first with side **A**, and then with side **B**. Check (√) the ones you read easily on side **B**. When a Memory Chip has three checks (√√√), put it in the **Words I Know** envelope.

1. THE PARTS OF A NEWSPAPER

Letter Groups   You know the words **ring** and **lock**. Find each of these words in one of the new words below. Circle the word you know in each word. Read the new words. Then write the new words on the lines.

bring _____clock _____

before   Circle the letter group **ore** in each word below. You know the first two words. Read and write the new word.

before   more   score _____

Base Word   You already know the word **interested**. This is the base word **interest** with an **ed** ending. Write the base word in the sentence below. Then read the sentence.

Does science _____you at all?

Take a Guess   Read the sentence below. See if you can guess the words in dark letters. Ask yourself, *What is a **star**? What would someone who is a star wear?*

The **movie** star is wearing fancy **clothes**.

Did you guess the words? Try another one: The shop was closed **yesterday**, but it's open for **business** today.

Write the four new words on the lines below.

_____ _____

_____ _____

Words to Know

	Look	Say	Picture	Write
basket bas-ket	☐	☐	☐	_____
bench	☐	☐	☐	_____
bring	☐	☐	☐	_____

	Look	Say	Picture	Write
business busi-ness	☐	☐	☐	_____
clock	☐	☐	☐	_____
clothes	☐	☐	☐	_____
event e-vent	☐	☐	☐	_____
fun	☐	☐	☐	_____
interest	☐	☐	☐	_____
less	☐	☐	☐	_____
movie mov-ie	☐	☐	☐	_____
score	☐	☐	☐	_____
state	☐	☐	☐	_____
yesterday yes-ter-day	☐	☐	☐	_____

Word Attack

+s Make new words by writing **s** after the words below. The word **business** already ends with **s**, so don't just add **s**, add **es**.

basket _____   break _____

bring _____   business _____

newspaper _____   buy _____

page _____   shut _____

team _____   space _____

event _____   movie _____

+ed These two words can take an **ed** ending. Write the new words. Then read the new words.

group _____ list _____

+ing Write **interest** with the ending **ing**. _____

2=1 You know the words **basket** and **ball**. Together, they make one new word. Write the word in the sentence below.

Dana plays _____ well.

1. THE PARTS OF A NEWSPAPER

A newspaper is not just a paper that brings you news. A newspaper brings you many other kinds of information as well. It is a tool you can use to help you live your life. To use this tool, you have to understand how it is put together. Every newspaper has different parts. Each part has a different kind of news or information.

The first part of a newspaper has what is called **hard news**. Hard news is any important or interesting event that has just happened. Many such events have to do with politics. But there are other kinds of hard news, too. A new President of the U.S.—that's hard news. A big storm that shuts down much of the city—that's hard news. A war that breaks out somewhere in the world—that's hard news, too. The most important news goes on the front page. Less important news goes on other pages inside.

A newspaper has different parts for different kinds of news. For example, all the news about your city and state may be in a part of its own. In most big-city newspapers, you will find all the news about money and jobs in one part. This news is of great interest to some people, but not to everyone.

Another part of the newspaper gives only sports news. Here, you can find out how all the teams did in every main sport. You can get the score for a basketball game yesterday. You can find out how many baskets each player had and who made the winning basket.

Still another part has articles about fun things to do and see around town. Do you want to know where to hear some music tonight? Do you want to know what big shows are coming to town? What movies are playing now? When and where to see a movie? You can find out from the newspaper.

Every newspaper has ads, too. A newspaper cannot keep going without ads. People and businesses pay to put ads in the newspaper. In fact, most of the money that a newspaper makes comes from ads.

There are, however, two kinds of ads in a newspaper. One kind is put in by businesses. These ads are found all through the newspaper. Some are big—they can take up a whole page. Some even take up two pages. Ads of this kind may have pictures and headings written in fancy letters. These ads try to make people stop and look. They give information that helps businesses sell things. This kind of ad may tell you of a clothes sale. It may tell you that the new cars for the year have come in. It may tell about some good buys down at the food store.

The other kind of ad is often known as a want ad. These are found in only one part of the paper. Want ads are very small. They are listed one after another in long lines. Some want ads tell of jobs that are open. Some tell of houses and apartments for sale or rent. Most want ads are taken out by people who have something for sale. If you want a used car or a used computer, the want ads are a good place to look. But anything else might turn up in the want ads, too. Are you looking for an old clock? Do you want to buy a used park bench? You may or may not find one in the want ads—but it's worth a look, anyway.

10

Finding Paragraphs

The sentences in a written work are grouped together. Each group is called a **paragraph**. A paragraph has only one main idea. All the sentences in the paragraph say something about this idea. You can tell where one paragraph ends and a new one starts just by looking at a page. Each new paragraph starts on a new line. It starts a few spaces in from the left side. Count the paragraphs in **Parts of a Newspaper**. How many do you find?

_____

Finding Main Idea Sentences

Sometimes, one sentence in a paragraph tells the main idea. Look at the second paragraph in **Parts of a Newspaper**. The first sentence tells you the main idea. It is that the first part of a newspaper is for hard news. This is a main-idea sentence. All the other sentences give some detail about hard news.

Now look at the third, fourth, and fifth paragraphs. Look for the main-idea sentence in each of these paragraphs. Write the main-idea sentences on the lines below.

Paragraph 3 _____

_____

_____

Paragraph 4 _____

_____

_____

Paragraph 5 _____

_____

_____

2. DANA ON HER OWN

When Dana was young, her family moved to a place just outside the city. She has lived outside the city most of her life. Now she is 18 years old and has finished high school. She wants to move back to the city and start a life of her own. Her family likes the idea and is willing to help her any way they can. But Dana doesn't want a lot of help. That's just the point. She wants to do things on her own now.

One day, she runs into Jen. Dana and Jen were good friends in high school. Jen is a year older than Dana. She got out of school last year. She has a part-time job and takes college classes. Later, she and another woman rented an apartment in the city. But the other woman has just moved out. Jen can't handle the rent by herself. She is looking for someone to move in with her.

"Say, how about you?" she says to Dana. "Would you be interested? The bedroom is big, and it gets a lot of sun. We have a big kitchen and living room, and the neighborhood is safe. Your part of the rent would come to $405. What do you think?"

"What do I think? I think it's a great idea," says Dana. That same week, Dana moves her things into the new place.

She doesn't have much—just her clothes. She will need a lot of things now that she is on her own. She starts to write down all the things she will need. Then it hits her that she can't buy any of these things—not yet. She will need some money first. To get some money, she will need a job. To get a job, she will have to go around town from business to business. To get around town, she will need a car. To get a car, she will need money. To get money—

"Wait," she says, "I'm back to where I started. First things first, they say—but what if there is no first thing? This is all one big circle."

"Look," says Jen, "you don't need a car at first. You can get around the city on a bus. Buy yourself a pass. With that, you can ride any bus, anytime, from anywhere to anywhere. You keep your mind on getting a job. You will need it to pay the rent! Go out and buy a newspaper. Look through the want ads. See what there is."

"Right away," says Dana. She changes to street clothes and heads off. On the way to the corner, she remembers that she will need some change. She looks through her bag. All she has are dollar bills. Will she have to go all the way back to the apartment? She turns. A guy is coming up behind her. He has to stop short so as not to crash into her. "Do you happen to have change for a dollar?" she asks.

He does not seem to even see her. He seems to be looking at something past her. Yet, he looks through his pocket and finds some change. He gives it to her and takes her dollar. Dana moves on.

Getting to Know Characters

So far you know two characters by name in this story. Write their names in the chart below. Write the name of the main character on the first line to the left. Write the name of the other character on the line below it.

Names of characters	Facts about the characters
_____	_____
	_____
	_____
	_____
_____	_____
	_____
	_____
	_____

Write three facts about each character in the chart. Use facts from the box below.

Is one year older	Just finished high school
Is living on her own	Wants to live on her own
Never lived in the city	Has a job

Writing a Plot Summary

The sentences below all tell things that have happened so far in this story. Use six of them to write a summary of what has happened so far. Remember that a summary tells only main events. So leave out sentences that give small details.

Dana runs into Jen, an old friend from high school.
Jen is taking classes at a college.
Jen asks Dana to move in with her.
She says the kitchen and living room of the apartment are big.
Dana is not sure where to start in setting up her new life.
Jen tells Dana to work on getting a job first of all.
Dana says, "Right away."
Dana goes out to buy a newspaper.
On the way, she takes change from a young man.

_____

_____

_____

_____

_____

_____

Finding the Main Idea

Each paragraph in a story has one main idea. But the story as a whole has one bigger main idea. Read these sentences about **Dana On Her Own**. Which one best tells the main idea of the whole story so far?

Dana moves into the city to start a life of her own.
Dana meets an old friend from high school.
Dana meets a boy on the way to the corner.

_____

_____

3. SHOPPING THE WANT ADS

Letter Groups   You know the first two words in each set of words below. The last word—the one in dark letters—is new. Circle the letter group that all three words in the set share. Then read the new word and write it on the line.

pack   back   **black**   _____

lock   rock   **block**   _____

team   scream   **dream**   _____

pick   stick   **quick**   _____

Take a Guess   Read the sentence below. The words in dark letters are new. Try to guess these words. The words **car** and **hear** should help you.

The **engine** in that car is so **loud** that you can hear it for miles!

Did you guess the two new words? Now write them on the lines below.

_____   _____

Words to Know

	Look	Say	Picture	Write
add	☐	☐	☐	_____
aunt	☐	☐	☐	_____
black	☐	☐	☐	_____
block	☐	☐	☐	_____
dream	☐	☐	☐	_____
engine en-gine	☐	☐	☐	_____
example ex-am-ple	☐	☐	☐	_____

16

	Look	Say	Picture	Write
loud	☐	☐	☐	_____
model mod-el	☐	☐	☐	_____
number num-ber	☐	☐	☐	_____
power pow-er	☐	☐	☐	_____
quick	☐	☐	☐	_____
special spe-cial	☐	☐	☐	_____
uncle un-cle	☐	☐	☐	_____

Word Attack

+s   Write the words below with **s** at the end.

block _____ school _____

room _____ slow _____

ad _____

+er   Add the ending **er** to **dark**. _____

Add the ending **er** to **storm**. _____

+ly   Add the ending **ly** to **quick**. _____

+ing   You can put the ending **ing** on **let**. You have to add one more **t** to **let**. Write the new word.

let (+t) + ing = _____

2=1   The word **playground** is made up of two words you know. Read this new word. Write the words that are in it.

playground = _____ + _____

+'s   **Bill** can be a name. To show that **Bill** owns or has something, add **'s** at the end. Write the new word in the sentence below.

Hey, isn't this _____ house?

3. SHOPPING THE WANT ADS

Want ads in a newspaper are grouped together. All the ads for jobs will be in one place. All the apartments for rent will be under another heading. Houses for rent will make up another group. Houses for sale will show up under yet another heading. Then there are all the different kinds of things people want to buy and sell. Cars might make up one group. Computers make up another.

When you shop the want ads, look at the headings first. These are in darker, bigger letters. Each one may be inside a box. Use the headings to help you find the group of ads you are interested in. Then look through this group for the very thing you want.

Sometimes, want ads can be hard to understand. People have to pay for these ads by the word—or even by the letter. They don't want to use any more letters than they have to. At the same time, they want to pack in as much information as they can. So they leave out words not needed to get their idea across. Sometimes, they use just one or two letters to stand for a whole word. They may write **nu** for **new**—just to save a letter. They may write **rms** for **rooms** or **apt** for **apartment**. Because of this, you sometimes have to work a little to guess what a want ad means.

To help you guess, ask yourself what the ad is for. This will point you to the kind of information you should find. Just about any car ad will tell you what year the car was made. It will tell you the make and model of the car. The ad may tell you how many miles the car has on it. It is sure to tell how much money the owner is asking. It may tell what new parts, if any, the car has. Also, it gives a number to call if you are interested. Look at this ad.

'97 Stormer, black.
Runs gd, looks great! 60K miles.
power+! $1400. Call 555-5555.

In this ad, **'97** stands for the year 1997. **Stormer** is, of course, the make of the car. The letters **gd** stand for **good**. But what does **60K** mean? It means **60,000**. The letter **K** is often used to stand for **1,000**. **Power +** is a way of letting you know that the car has a strong engine.

An ad about an apartment for rent will give another whole set of information. It will tell you how big the place is, how much the rent is, and who to call. It may give other information, too. It may tell something about the neighborhood. It may tell you things you can or can't do there. Look at this ad.

> **$575 5-room dream apt.**
> **Close to schools. One block to playground;**
> **two blocks to bus. No loud music. Dogs OK.**
> **Call 555-5555 after 6. Ask for Mr. White.**

An ad for a job will tell what the job is, who you will work for, and what special skills you may need. Sometimes, it tells how much money you will get. More often you have to find out about the money when you go in to see about the job. Here is an ad for a job.

COOK:
Uncle Bill's fast-food
restaurant needs full-time cook.
Great pay. Call 555-5555 between
2–10 PM.

Reading for Facts

Sometimes, it is best to read every word and think about each sentence. But not always. If you are looking for just one detail or fact, you may want to read in a different way. You let your eye move over the page quickly. In this way, you read just enough of each line to see if it has the information you need. If not, you move on.

Try out this way of reading. Look through **Shopping the Want Ads**. Find an ad for a car. Then find the answer to each question below. Write each answer on the line.

What year is the car? _____

How much is the owner asking for it? _____

How many miles are there on the car? _____

What number should you call? _____

Now find the ad that tells about an apartment for rent. Answer these questions about the apartment.

How big is the apartment? _____

How much is the rent? _____

What is it close to? _____

Can you live there if you own a dog? _____

What number should you call? _____

Who should you ask for? _____

Now find the ad about a job. Answer the two questions.

What kind of work is it? _____

When should you call? _____

4. NEW IN THE CITY

Dan is new in the city. All through high school, he lived with his family in a small town about 75 miles north of the city. After high school, he didn't know what to do with his life. He could have gone back to a job he had the summer before—cooking at a fast-food place down by the freeway. But he doesn't want that job anymore. It doesn't pay enough, and it seems like a job for a kid. Dan feels he is no longer a kid. In his town, there are hardly any jobs for a young man. So Dan did a lot of nothing in his first summer out of high school. At first he liked it, but that way of life can get old fast.

One night, his uncle called from the city. Dan's uncle works for a business called Henson Homes. They build houses. Dan's uncle said that a job was about to open up at his place of work. It was not a great job. It did not call for any special skills. Most of the time, Dan would be helping out in the office.

"But," said his uncle, "the pay is OK. I'm sure it's better than anything you can get in your town, Dan. You can learn on this job. You can pick up some job skills. You like computers, don't you? Well, you would run a computer here. You'll make out bills. You can learn how to keep books for a business. What's more, Henson Homes is starting to grow. If you are a hard worker, you can move up as time goes on. Are you interested? I could put in a word for you."

Dan said he was very interested. The next week, his uncle called to say he had the job.

So Dan lives in the city now. Moving here was a big change, as it turns out. Maybe it was a little more change than he was looking for. He still feels lost here most of the time. But he is excited, too. Every day seems full of adventures. Every time he leaves the house, he feels as if anything could happen.

Today, he is going to the corner to buy a newspaper. He needs to look at the want ads. Dan is still living with his aunt and uncle, and that can't last. Their place is not big enough. Dan wants a place of his own.

On the way, a young woman pushes past him, going fast. She has a red hat and dark glasses. She is looking through her bag as she walks. Suddenly, she stops and turns. "Do you have change for a dollar?" she asks Dan.

"Sure." Dan gives her the change and takes the dollar bill from her hand. The girl walks on. When he gets to the newspaper box on the corner, he finds himself in line behind her. She uses the change she took from Dan to buy a paper. Then it's Dan's turn to buy a paper.

He opens the paper. He can't wait to look through the want ads. So he goes into a restaurant on the corner, buys a cool drink, and finds a place to sit. The girl with the dark glasses is in the same restaurant, sitting by herself.

Dan opens his paper to the want ads. He starts to look at apartments for rent. Most of them are too much money for Dan. One time, when he looks up, he sees that the girl has taken off her dark glasses. She, too, has her paper open to the want ads. *Now, what could she be looking for?* he asks himself. *Could she be new in town—like me?* he wants to ask her. She does not seem interested in making new friends. So he looks back at his own newspaper.

This time his eye happens to land on an interesting ad under **Apartments for Rent.** This is the ad:

$300: Big apartment. 3 rooms.
New building. Quiet and sunny.
All-electric kitchen. Call Mack, 555-5555.

This looks great! Maybe this will be his new place. Dan wants to tell someone. He looks around for the girl with the red hat. But she is gone.

Finding the Main Idea

As you know, a paragraph is a group of sentences about the same main idea. Sometimes, the main idea is right there in one of the sentences. More often, the main idea is not in any one sentence. You can tell what the main idea is from looking at all the sentences that are there. You can see that all the sentences point toward one idea, or all the sentences together add up to one idea. Look at the first paragraph of **New in the City**. The main idea of this paragraph could be put as follows:

Dan couldn't find a good job in his hometown.

Every sentence in the paragraph adds some little piece to this main idea. Some tell when he couldn't find a good job (after high school). Some tell why he didn't want the job he could find (doesn't pay enough, and so on). Some tell why he can't find a good job (no jobs for a young man). Some tell where his hometown is (75 miles north of the city). All the sentences together add up to the main idea.

Now look at the second paragraph of the story. Which of the sentences below best gives the main idea of this whole paragraph? Circle the sentence.

Dan's uncle told him about a job in the city.

One night, a great thing happened.

Dan likes to talk to his uncle.

Try one more. Look at the third paragraph of the story. Now read the sentences below. Pick the one that best tells the main idea of the third paragraph. Circle it.

His uncle tells him about Henson Homes.

Dan finds out he can run a computer on this job.

His uncle tells him some good things about the job.

Alike and Different

You read about Dana in **Dana On Her Own.** Now you have read about Dan. In some ways, these two characters are **in the same boat.** In some ways, they face different problems. Look at each fact below. Write **Dan** if it tells only about Dan. Write **Dana** if it tells only about Dana. Write **Both** if it tells something about both characters.

_____ just finished high school

_____ wants to start a new life in the city

_____ is young

_____ needs a car

_____ was living just outside the city

_____ is moving away from home for the first time

_____ already has a place to live

_____ was living in a small town north of the city

_____ already has a job

_____ needs a place to live

_____ needs a job

5. READING DIRECTIONS

Try This   You know how the letter group **ove** sounds in **move** and **prove**. This letter group sounds differently in **love**. Try both ways in this new word: **above**. What is the word? Write it in this sentence.

Most of the building is _____ the ground.

Letter Groups   You know the word **other**. Put **br** before **other**, and you have the new word: **brother**. Can you read this word? Write it in the sentence.

This is my sister, and that is my _____.

Read each set of words below. The word in dark letters is new. All the words in the same line share a letter group. Circle the letter group. Read the new word and then write it in the space.

joke   **smoke**   _____

those   **suppose**   _____

dark   park   **mark**   _____

before   explore   more   **store**   _____

Take a Guess   The word **once** is made from **one**. Look for this new word in the sentence below. See if you can guess what it means from the rest of the sentence. The words **not**, **but**, and **two** should help you.

Mu Lan went to California not **once** but two times.

Write the new word. _____

Words to Know

	Look	Say	Picture	Write
above a-bove	☐	☐	☐	_____
brother broth-er	☐	☐	☐	_____
easy eas-y	☐	☐	☐	_____
hour	☐	☐	☐	_____
mark	☐	☐	☐	_____
minute min-ute	☐	☐	☐	_____
once	☐	☐	☐	_____
second sec-ond	☐	☐	☐	_____
step	☐	☐	☐	_____
store	☐	☐	☐	_____
suppose sup-pose	☐	☐	☐	_____
table ta-ble	☐	☐	☐	_____

Word Attack

+s   Write each word below with an **s** ending.

tool _____food _____

hour _____piece _____

minute _____step _____

hang _____

+ing   Add the ending **ing** to **miss**. _____
Add the ending **ing** to **pull**. _____

+ed   You can add the **ed** ending to each of the words below. The word **suppose** already has an **e** at the end, so just add **d.**

burn _____ suppose _____

+er   Write **young** with an **er** ending in the sentence below.

My brother is _____ than I am.

+'s   As you know, you can add the ending **'s** to show that someone owns or has something. Add **'s** to these words.

boy _____ kid _____

Now use the two new words in this sentence.

They found a _____ bike in that _____ house.

Write **uncle** with **'s** at the end. _____

1+1   The words **there is** can be written as one new word: **there's**. Write the new word on the line below. Then circle the letters you left out of the two words to write the one word.

there is = _____

5. READING DIRECTIONS

Suppose your younger brother comes to you with a problem. He has a new bike—but it is all in pieces. Can you put it together for him? "It's easy," you say. "Just follow the directions."

Well, maybe it is not so easy. Written directions are a fact of life—you come across them every day. But even well-written directions can be hard to follow. Many directions are not well written.

Here are some points that can help you follow any directions you come across. First, start by looking through the whole set of directions from start to finish one time. Don't try to follow them at this point. Just read for the big picture. Get an idea of how the whole job should go.

Most directions have two parts. One part tells what things you will need. Another part tells what you should do. After you read the whole set of directions once, read the first part again. When you finish this part, stop and see if you have everything you need.

If you are cooking something, the directions will start with a list of foods. Set these on a table so you can see what you have. If there's anything you need from the store, get it now.

Suppose you are putting together a bike. The first part of the directions tell what tools you need and what parts are supposed to be in the box. It may even show a picture of the parts. After you finish reading the first part of the directions, stop. Get your tools together. Make sure you have all the parts shown. If something is missing, this is the time to go back to the store.

After you finish pulling your tools together, read the second part of the directions. Now it's time to follow the directions step by step. It's important to go one step at a time. Read each step, do that step, and then go on to the next one. Mark your place after you finish reading so that you can come back to the same place each time. That way you won't miss any steps. Above all, take your time. A job may take minutes if you are slow and hours if you are fast. Why? Because when you move too fast, you often do some things wrong.

Follow the steps in the order that they are written. Good directions will give you the steps in the right order. When you finish the last step, the kid's bike should be ready to ride. Or, if you were cooking, set the table—it's time to eat.

Some directions don't tell how to make something. They tell how to get from one place to another. Directions of this kind don't have a first part—the tools you will need. They only have part two—the steps you should take. Most of the time, you don't see these directions written out. You hear them—over the telephone more often than not. If you want to remember them, you have to write them down. Your main problem, then, is to write the directions in such a way that you can understand and follow them later.

You may not have time to take down every word as you are listening to the directions. Just be sure to get the most important ones. Suppose you want to go to your uncle's house. You call him up. He tells you, "Take the freeway north, get off at Main Street, and go two blocks—" Then he hangs up. You might write, *Freeway N, Main, 2.* As soon as you hang up the telephone, look at what you have written. Write the directions over again—right away while you still remember what was said. Remember that you will have to read your own writing later, so make sure that you'll know what every word means.

Following Directions

The article you have just read tells how to follow directions. Use the information in the article to fill in the directions below. First, find the best ending for each step. Next, circle the letter of the ending you have picked (**a**, **b**, or **c**). Then, write the missing words in the space that follows the step.

How to Follow Directions

1. For any kind of directions, start by

    a. doing what the first step tells you.
    b. reading the directions from start to finish once.
    c. going to the store.

    _____

    _____

2. If the directions are for making something,

    a. read the first part again and then stop.
    b. read through the whole set again.
    c. go right to the store and get what you need.

    _____

    _____

3. After reading the first part again,

    a. get together all the tools and other things you will need.
    b. go right on to part two.
    c. ask for help if you need it.

    _____

    _____

4. Next,

    a. read the rest of the directions to the end.
    b. follow part two of the directions, one step at a time.
    c. follow the directions two steps at a time.

    _____

    _____

5. If you are taking down directions for going somwhere,

    a. write down every other word.
    b. write down every word.
    c. write down every important word.

    _____

    _____

6. After you hang up the telephone,

    a. put the directions in your pocket till
       you need them.
    b. call the person back.
    c. look at the directions right away and
       write them over.

    _____

    _____

6. DAN TAKES THE BUS

Dan thinks he has found an apartment that will be just right for him. He calls the number given in the ad. A man answers.

"Hi," says Dan. "I am calling about your ad in the paper."

"The dog has already been sold," the man says.

Before the man can hang up, Dan says, "No, wait! I was calling about an apartment. Is this the right number?"

"Oh—the apartment. Yes, this is the right number. But let me tell you, I am not going to rent it to just anyone. Have you got a job?"

"Yes," says Dan.

"All right," says the man. "How old are you?"

"Well—almost 19."

"You're 18," says the man. "I suppose you like loud music, do you?"

"Well," says Dan, "maybe sometimes. But could I—"

"OK, OK," the man cuts in, "you can look at the place. You're not the only one who wants it, you know. A lot of people are coming today. I'm not going to hold it for you or anyone. Get here fast, and have your money ready." He gives Dan directions for getting there on the bus. But he talks fast, and Dan has to write quickly.

Later, standing on Main Street waiting for the bus, he looks at the directions. Oh, no! What are all these words and letters he has written? What do they mean? Here is what he sees: **156N, Cruz, left 3, right 1, up, woods (not) 1453**

Then he remembers one thing. **156** is the bus line. Cruz? Yes, he remembers something about that, too. The man told him to get off at Cruz Street. Well, that's all he needs for now. He can call again when he gets to Cruz Street.

The bus comes, and Dan gets on. At this time of day, there are not many people on the bus. Dan sits by a window and reads street names as he moves along. The bus keeps going, and he never sees Cruz Street. At last, he calls to the bus driver. "What happened to Cruz Street? Is it coming up soon?"

"Cruz Street is back the other way, my friend—way back!" the driver laughs.

Dan looks at his directions again. He sees the letter **N** for the first time. Suddenly, he knows what the **N** stands for: north. He took the right bus, but going the wrong way. At the next stop, he gets off, walks across the street, and waits for the bus again.

This time he gets on the **156** going north. He asks the bus driver to let him know when they get close to Cruz Street. The bus goes right past the place where Dan started. That's when the driver calls out, "Cruz Street coming up!"

Dan was only two blocks south of Cruz when he started out! So it has taken him an hour to go two blocks by bus. He could have walked to the apartment in 10 minutes, and he would have saved a dollar!

Remembering Details

Dan has trouble finding his way to the apartment he wants to rent. Here are some sentences about Dan's bad day. One word is missing from each sentence. The missing words are in the box. Write the word that goes in each space. Look back at the story if you need to.

north   Cruz   south   north   Cruz   Main   south

1. Dan waits for the bus on _____Street.

2. He wants to take the bus to _____Street.

3. Dan starts out just _____of Cruz street.

4. He gets on a bus going _____.

5. Dan gets off and waits for a bus going _____.

6. He goes two blocks _____of where he started.

7. There, he finds _____Street at last!

What Do You Think?

One of the sentences above tells the thing that Dan did wrong. Circle the sentence. Now talk about the story with one or more friends who have read it. Why did Dan have this problem. What might he have done to make sure this wouldn't happen?

7. FILLING OUT FORMS

Break It Up   You can find two words you know in the new word **ago**. The smaller words are **a** and **go**. They don't tell you what the bigger word means. But they can help you read the word. Try reading it now: **ago**. Write the new word in the sentence below, and read the sentence.

This place was different many years _____.

Letter Groups   You know the first two words below. The last word is new. But all three words end with the same letter group. Circle that letter group. Read the new word which is in darker letters. Then write it on the line.

pick   stick   **trick** _____

Take a Guess   Read the sentences below. See if you can guess the word in dark letters.

A **month** is four weeks long.

Did you guess the word? Write it. _____

Words to Know

	Look	Say	Picture	Write
ago a-go	☐	☐	☐	
buzzer buzz-er	☐	☐	☐	_____
company com-pa-ny	☐	☐	☐	_____
correct cor-rect	☐	☐	☐	_____
doctor doc-tor	☐	☐	☐	_____
empty emp-ty	☐	☐	☐	_____
month	☐	☐	☐	_____

	Look	Say	Picture	Write
parents par-ents	☐	☐	☐	_____
person per-son	☐	☐	☐	_____
security se-cu-ri-ty	☐	☐	☐	_____
trick	☐	☐	☐	_____

Word Attack

+s Write these words with **s**. Read the new words.

brother _____ chance _____

number _____ paper _____

stay _____ person _____

+ly Add the ending **ly** to each of the words below.

careful _____ close _____

correct _____

+ing Write these words with an **ing** ending.

fill _____ grow _____

7. FILLING OUT FORMS

Do you want to take the driver's test? First, you will have to fill out a form. Do you want to try for a job at some big company? First, you will have to fill out a form. Do you feel sick? Do you need to see a doctor? Guess what? You have to fill out a form.

Many years ago, you could get through your whole life and never see a form, but those days are gone. Filling out forms is now a growing part of day-to-day life.

How can you be sure to fill out a form correctly? First, you need to know one thing. A form does not ask questions for the most part. It gives you headings. You are supposed to fill in the information that goes under each heading.

It is important to read a form carefully. Why? Because filling out a form really comes down to following directions. Almost every form asks for your full name. Now, in day-to-day life, you would write your first name first, your middle name next, and your last name last. But look closely at the form. Do you see some small headings just above, below, or next to the lines on which you are to write your name? Do they say **Last**, **First**, and **Middle**? These headings show the order in which you should write your name. The form may ask that you write your last name first, your first name second, and your middle name last. Whatever the form asks for, that's what you should do.

Here and there on a form, you may see special directions. Follow these, too. There may be a box with the words, **For office use only**. Leave a box like that empty. Or the directions may say, **Answer questions 1-13**. If that is what the form says, don't answer question 14. Make sure you understand each question, too. If the form has a name with a space after it, should you write your name? Look again. What if that part of the form is asking about your parents? If the form says brothers, don't write their names. Maybe the form just wants a number—it may be asking how many, not who. Just be careful. You're not in a race, and you don't have to beat a buzzer. Take your time.

Some questions turn up on many different forms. You almost always have to write down where you live, when you were born, and what your telephone number is. Often, you are asked to name someone who knows you well and to give a telephone number for this person (or persons). Another number you may have to write on a form is your social security number. You might write some of this information on a card and keep it with you. Then when you have to fill out a form, you will have the correct information at hand.

Also, there are some important numbers that you should not keep on yourself. Many people have money in the bank. They have a special number for their card for the bank machine. It's OK to write down this number, but keep the written number at home with other important papers. Don't take it with you when you go out. That way, even if your bank card falls into the wrong hands, your money stays in the bank.

Fill Out a Form

The form below asks for information about the article you have just read. Use the information in the article to fill out the form correctly.

Answer question 1 and questions 3-7.
DO NOT ANSWER QUESTION 2.

1. Name: _____ _____ _____

2. Your telephone number: _____

3. Birth date: _____ _____ _____

4. Date when article was read: _____ _____ ____
                                         Day   Month   Year

5. Name of article: _____

6. Number of paragraphs:
_____

7. What article is about: (Circle the letter of your answer.)

    a.   How to fill out forms

    b.   How to follow directions

    c.   How to keep your papers safe

    d.   How to cook

Do not write in this space
   Name
   Number
   Street
   CRX _____ QTB _____ TT - YY - GG _____

8. A GREAT APARTMENT

Dan has gone up one street and down another. He has turned left, and he has turned right. Now he looks again at his directions. He sees the words: **Woods (not)**.

He looks up and—well, well! Right next to the street is a little green space, about two feet by six feet. It has a few little plants. In front of it is a sign that says, **The Woods**.

Not, thinks Dan. *Good, I must be close.* Just then he sees the building up ahead. It is an old, green building. It looks like it is about to fall down.

No one answers Dan's ring. He tries the handle—the door is open. He walks in. "Hi!" he calls out. "Anyone here?"

A man sticks his head out of a door. "You called about the apartment?"

"I'm the one," says Dan.

"Follow me."

Dan follows the man down the hall. On the telephone, the man had said that many people were interested in the apartment. But they do not seem to be here now. Dan hears music from one apartment. He hears voices from another. Two people seem to be having a bad fight. This place is loud!

"Here we are," says the man, and he throws open a door.

Dan walks in and looks around. He sees just one room, and it is not very big. It has two small windows, but the room is pretty dark. "Didn't the ad say three rooms?" Dan asks.

"You got your kitchen over there," says the man, and he points to the corner.

"But that's not another room!" says Dan. "That's just a corner of this room. Anyway, the ad said, **all-electric kitchen**! What about that part?"

"There is electricity in that corner," says the man.

Dan is getting a bad feeling about this apartment. "Where is room three?" he wants to know. "Don't tell me. It's the other corner."

"Of course not. Look." The man opens a door that Dan did not happen to see till now. Behind it is a dark space with no windows at all. "You can sleep in there," says the man. "The last guy did. It's quiet."

"What?" cries Dan. "That's not a room!"

"If it's big enough to sleep in, it's a room. You interested? Sign here." The man sticks out a form. Dan looks through the form. Then he turns it over. On the back he sees some words in small letters. The words say that he must stay in the apartment for a year.

"Does the $300 pay for electricity and water?" he asks.

"No, that will run you $40 more. Then, of course, I have to ask for another $10 to keep the hall clean," says the man.

"Do you mean you want $350 in all? How can you ask that much for a place like this?" Dan can't believe what he hears.

"You get what you pay for," says the man.

"Not here, you don't," says Dan. "I'm not interested. Forget it."

"Hey!" The man follows him to the door. "By the time you change your mind, it will be too late. A lot of people want this apartment. It will be gone by tonight!"

But Dan just leaves. On the way to Main Street, he sees a sign in a window: **Room for rent**.

A woman lets him into this new building. "You have a room for rent?" Dan asks.

"Sure. It's up the stairs. Follow me." The woman shows Dan one big room with a really big window. A door on one wall opens into a small, clean kitchen.

"How much?" Dan asks.

"$300 a month," she says. "That takes care of everything— electricity, water, the works."

"This is great!" says Dan. "When can I move in?"

"Fill out the form," says the woman. "You look like a quiet young man. If you can prove you have a job, you can move into the room."

Dan has all the information the woman needs. He can—and does—fill out the form right then and there. He has the money, too. Soon, he finds himself alone in his own apartment! He stands by the big window in the empty room and looks down at the street. Suddenly, a woman steps out of the building across the way. Dan puts his head close to the glass to get a better look. She is wearing a red hat. It's the girl he saw on the way to buy a newspaper. Has he moved in across the street from her? Dan throws open the window and sticks his head out. He wants to call out to her. Then he remembers that he doesn't even know her name. So he doesn't call out after all.

Finding Details

In this story, Dan looks at two apartments. He has read about the first one in the want ads. Points from the ad are listed on the left. Next to each point, write what the apartment is really like.

Big   The apartment is _____.

3 rooms   The apartment really has_____.

$300   The rent is really_____.

Quiet   The apartment is really _____.

Sunny   The apartment is really _____.

New building   The apartment is in _____.

All-electric kitchen   The kitchen is _____.

Alike and Different

Dan sees a sign for the second apartment on his way to Main Street. Each sentence below tells how the second apartment is different from the first one. Fill in the missing word. Pick one of the two words below each sentence.

The second apartment is _____.
(bigger/smaller)

The second apartment gets _____light.
(more/less)

The second apartment has a _____kitchen.
(real/smaller)

The second apartment is _____money.
(more/not as much)

9. UNDERSTANDING ADS

Try This   The vowel group **oo** can sound many different ways. It sounds one way in **foot**, another way in **floor**. Now look at the word: **shoot**. You know the sound of **sh** at the beginning and **t** at the end. Try three different sounds for **oo** till you get a word that would be right in the sentence below. Read the new word, **shoot**, and write it in the sentence.

Will likes to _____ pictures of his family.

Letter Groups   In each group of words below, you know the first two words. The word in dark letters is new. It ends with the same letter group as the first two. Circle the letter group you find in all the words. Read the new word and write it on the line.

map	trap	**clap**	_____
card	hard	**guard**	_____
slow	below	**low**	_____
stairs	fair	**pair**	_____
hot	plot	**shot**	_____

Take a Guess   Read the sentences below. See if you can guess the word in dark letters. The word **basketball** should help you. Think about where the game of basketball is played.

The basketball player steps onto the **court**.

Did you guess the word? Now write it. _____

Words to Know

	Look	Say	Picture	Write
clap	☐	☐	☐	_____
court	☐	☐	☐	_____
crowd	☐	☐	☐	_____
guard	☐	☐	☐	_____
jump	☐	☐	☐	_____
low	☐	☐	☐	_____
moment mo-ment	☐	☐	☐	_____
pair	☐	☐	☐	_____
price	☐	☐	☐	_____
rule	☐	☐	☐	_____
shoot	☐	☐	☐	_____
shot	☐	☐	☐	_____
slam	☐	☐	☐	_____

Word Attack

+s Write these words with an **s** ending. Add **e** to pass before you add **s**.

pass _____   rule _____

second _____   slam _____

trick _____   wear _____

your _____   jump _____

score _____   shoot _____

street _____   face _____

+ed Another ending you can add to **pass** is **ed**. Write this new word in the sentence below.

Tom _____ the ball to me.

+ing   Write the words below with the ending **ing**. Add one more **p** to **clap** before you add **ing**.

clap _____ guard _____

shoot _____ understand _____

2=1   Each of the words below is made up of two words. Circle the two words in each word. Then write each whole word on the line and read it out loud.

sunglasses _____ themselves _____

+'s   Add **'s** to **spider** to show that the **spider** has something.

spider + 's = _____

1+1   You can write the two words **he will** as one word: **he'll**.

   Write the two words in the first sentence below. Write the one word in the second sentence.

Dan says _____ _____ be back. In fact, _____
be back soon.

The words **were not** can be written as one word: **weren't**. Write the two words in the first sentence below. Write the one word in the second sentence.

The girls _____ _____ happy.

They _____ happy at all!

9. UNDERSTANDING ADS

Some ads are full of facts—and the facts may be correct. But giving facts is not the point of most ads. The main point of most ads is to sell something. The ad tries to make you want the thing it is selling. So it tries to get to your feelings in some way. If it gives you facts, it hides some other ideas in with the facts. Take a look at this example.

This ad does have three facts in it. Here they are:

1. Spider's Sun Shop sells Explorer sunglasses.
2. One pair of these glasses goes for $39.95.
3. Two pairs go for $78.99.

That's it. All the other words in the ad are just there to get to your feelings. The ad says the shop is going to **break the rules** today. That sounds exciting. But what does it mean? Nothing, really. There is no rule against a shop having a sale. The ad says you have been waiting for this sale. But have you? How would Spider's Sun Shop know? Is $39.95 such a low, LOW, LOW price? Maybe yes, maybe no. You can't tell just from this ad. You have to ask how much they were before the sale, and how much they are in other shops. What if you can get them for $20 somewhere else? Then the price here is not so low, LOW, LOW.

To see the information in an ad, you have to see through the words. No one really wants to be left out or left behind. People want to be in the middle of things—part of the group. So an ad may say something like this: Hey, what are you waiting for? You want to be the last one in the world to get some really cool Explorer sunglasses? Get with it! Join the gang! Buy a pair of Explorers before life has passed you by.

On the other hand, most people like to think they are special. They like to think of themselves as one-of-a-kind. An ad may try to reach this side of people. Picture an ad for Explorer sunglasses on TV. You see a man on a mountain. He is all alone. Then you see him up close. He is wearing sunglasses. Suddenly, he turns and faces you. He says, "I've tried all those other sunglasses. They might work for other people—not for me. I make up my own mind. I go my own way. Explorers—they're the only sunglasses for me." He turns and walks away. A voice says, "Explorer sunglasses: they're not for everyone."

An ad like that will make some people want Explorer sunglasses. These are people who want to stand out in a crowd. Of course, if the ad really works, a crowd of people will soon be wearing the glasses. So the very thing that makes the ad work, soon makes it wrong. Right?

Let's say you turn on the TV and see the best point guard who ever lived. If you love basketball, you become excited. You want to clap. There he is on the court, making one of his great moves. He jumps! He shoots! He gets the ball back. He slams it through the basket. He scores again! You remember the time he won a championship at the last moment with a slam like that. His shot beat the buzzer by two seconds. Shooting 30 points a night is nothing for this guy. Guarding him is a bad dream. If only you could be more like him! Now as he comes down, he passes the ball off and turns. The great star gives you a cool smile. He puts on a pair of Explorer sunglasses. "I like these sunglasses," he says. Then the words show up on the TV: **EXPLORERS: the sunglasses that champions wear.**

An ad like this can really get to some people. Many people, after all, want to be like famous stars. They want to hear people clapping. They want to feel the eyes of the world on their every move. But wearing what some star wears won't bring about this change. If you buy Explorer sunglasses, all you'll get are glasses.

Understanding Main Ideas

Understanding Ads talks about some of the ways that ads try to trick people. Each way counts on different feelings that most people have. The three main feelings talked about in this article are listed below. Finish each sentence (**a**, **b**, and **c**) by writing one of the three endings given for it.

a. People want to be _____
   part of the group.
   better than the group.
   free from the group.

b. People want to feel that _____
   they are no one special.
   they are special.
   no one is special.

c. People want to be the same as _____
   their boss at work.
   their parents.
   famous stars.

Understanding Ads

The lines below come from different ads. Each ad tries to get to one of the feelings listed above. Next to each ad, write the letter of the feeling (**a**, **b**, or **c**).

_____ 1. "I just love a Gold Medal TV dinner after a long hard day on the set," says Jen Green, star of **Streets of Gold**.

_____ 2. Run, don't walk, to see **They Weren't So Bad After All**. It is the movie the whole country is talking about!

_____ 3. You're in a class by yourself. Step up to the car that is in a class by itself.

10. A GOOD USED CAR

Dan wants to buy a good used car. He thinks he'll have to save up for awhile. But one day, he hears an ad on the radio. It is for a used car place called the Car Guys. The man in the ad sounds so excited as he says, "Hey! Fast Jake here for the Car Guys. Come on over to the Car Guys! We're the guys who say YES! Yes, you can! YES, WE WILL! Yes, you do! YES! If you have a job, you can drive home a good used car tonight! YES, YOU CAN! Take a look at our Special of the Week. This is the Great One. Clean inside and out! LOW, LOW miles. Only one owner. What do you mean, you don't have money? You don't need MONEY to shop at the Car Guys. WE KNOW YOU! We LIKE you. We want to HELP you. We're the Car Guys! Put $100 down and take this monster machine home tonight!"

Dan thinks, *I have $100. Maybe I don't have to wait to buy a car. I could buy this Special of the Week right now.*

So he gets on a bus and goes over to the Car Guys. They have a big lot down by the freeway. It is full of used cars. All the cars look pretty good from far away. They all have signs that say things like **Special!** or **Great Buy!**

A man comes up and puts out his hand. "I'm Fast Jake. What can I do for you, my man?"

Dan says, "I heard your ad on the radio. I want to see that Special of the Week."

"Oh! Bad news! I just sold that one!" The man looks at his watch. "Oh, but hey! Good news! I have lots of other good buys. What kind of car are we looking for?"

"Well—just something I can count on," says Dan.

"I can get you into a very good little sports car for $5,500—"

"No, no—that's too much money," says Dan.

"How about a truck? I can sell you one for $3,000—"

"No, that's still too much," says Dan.

"OK, how about this little red two-door? It's a good city car. I drive one of these myself. I can let it go for $2,000." He walks Dan toward a red car. Just then, a young woman comes up to the car from the other side.

Dan can't believe his eyes. "Hey," he says to her, "I know you. Don't you live across the street from me?"

The woman takes off her sunglasses and gives Dan a close look. "What do you know! I do think I have seen you around. I'm Dana."

"I'm Dan. Were you interested in this car?"

"Yes, but you saw it first."

"No, no," says Dan, "you saw it first."

Fast Jake says, "Let me take the two of you out for a test drive. When you get back you can fight over the car."

So Dan and Dana take turns driving. The car feels good to Dan. He's ready to sign some papers. But Dana asks a lot of questions, and Dan listens to her. Fast Jake does not seem to know many answers. Back at the lot, Dana wants to look under the hood. After she has looked, she says, "Sorry, not for me. This car needs a ring job."

"A ring job!" Dan cries. "Isn't that like saying it needs a whole new engine?"

"Yes, something like that," says Dana.

"How do you know?"

Dana tells him all the signs she has seen. Fast Jake tries to cut in at first. But Dana knows what she is talking about. So after awhile, Fast Jake gives up.

Dan and Dana go home together on the bus that day. "How come you know so much about cars?" Dan asks.

Dana laughs. "I have been around cars all my life. Both my dad and my uncle fix cars for a living. They own a shop together."

"Oh, if only I had someone like you to help me buy a car," says Dan.

"Well," says Dana, "I could help you. I do have lots of time right now. I don't have a job."

"What's your number?" Dan asks.

Remembering Details

Write a detail from the story in each space below. Each detail can be one word or more than one word. Look back at the story if you need to.

Dan hears an ad on the _____. The ad says that he can get a good used car from the _____. The ad calls this good buy the _____.

When Dan goes to the used car place, he meets a man called _____. This man says the special has been sold, but he has a _____ for $5,500. Dan says that that's too much, so the man tells him about a truck for _____. That is still too much money for Dan, so Fast Jake shows him a little _____ two-door. Fast Jake says this is a good _____ car. Just then, a woman in sunglasses comes up to the same car. She says her name is _____. After a test drive, she asks to look under the _____. Then she says the car needs a _____ job. Later, on the bus, Dan asks how come she knows so much about _____. She tells him that her dad and her uncle own a _____ together. At the end, Dan asks for her _____.

11. JOBS

Try This   The vowel pair **oo** can sound many different ways. It sounds one way in **look** and **book**, another way in **cool** and **food**, and another way in **door** and **floor**. Which way does it sound in this word: **foot**? Try all three sounds till you hit a word you know.

Write the word. _____

Letter Groups   You know the first word in each pair below. The word in dark letters is new. Circle the letters that are the same in each pair. Read the new word, and write it in the sentence.

voice   **choice**   You have made a good _____.

pair   **hair**   Who cuts your _____?

Take a Guess   Read the sentences below. See if you can guess the words in dark letters.

The more you **practice**, the better you will be.
Forget about yesterday—get ready for **tomorrow**.

Write the new words. _____ _____

Words to Know

	Look	Say	Picture	Write
breath	☐	☐	☐	_____
calm	☐	☐	☐	_____
catch	☐	☐	☐	_____
center cen-ter	☐	☐	☐	_____
chance	☐	☐	☐	_____
choice	☐	☐	☐	_____
foot	☐	☐	☐	_____

54

	Look	Say	Picture	Write
forward for-ward	☐	☐	☐	_____
foster fos-ter	☐	☐	☐	_____
hair	☐	☐	☐	_____
interview in-ter-view	☐	☐	☐	_____
practice prac-tice	☐	☐	☐	_____
tomorrow to-mor-row	☐	☐	☐	_____

Word Attack

+s   Add **s** to the words below to make new words. Add **e** to **catch** before you add **s**.

catch_____   chance _____

choice _____   crowd _____

driver _____   forget_____

hurt _____   interview _____

listen _____   lose _____

love_____   mind _____

+ing   Write the words **learn** and **listen** with the ending **ing**.

learn _____listen _____

1+1   You can put the words **have** and **not** together into one word. Here is the word: **haven't**. Write the two words on the lines to the left below. Write the one word on the right. Circle the letters in **have not** that are left out of **haven't**.

_____ _____= _____

11. JOBS

Money: we all need it, and that's a fact. To get money, most of us need a job. But what kind of job? That's where the choices begin.

Some people think one job is just like another. Every job is different—and people are different, too. Some people like crowds. Others like to be alone. A job that is right for some people may be wrong for others.

So the first step in looking for a job is to look at yourself. What are you like? What do you do for fun? Questions like these can help you make the right choice. After all, it's best to go for a job that will interest you. That's the kind of job you have the best chance of getting. Your chances of keeping such a job are better, too.

Do you like to talk? Do you like to meet new people? Are you someone who never forgets a face? Maybe you belong in sales or in politics. Do you get along best with young kids? Think about a job in day care. Are people always coming to you with their problems? Are you good at listening? Many jobs center around helping other people. You might run a home for kids who are in trouble, or you might work at a home for older people.

Do you get along better with plants than with people? Any big office building has many plants. Taking care of them is a big job. Maybe it can be your job. If you can't stand to be inside all day, you might like a job in a park. Someone has to take care of those plants, too.

Some people like working with things better than with people. Do you like cars? It would take hours to list all the jobs that might interest you. You could sell cars. You could fix them. You could drive them—yes, there are jobs for drivers of all kinds. You could work on cars to help keep them running. The list goes on and on.

After you know what kind of job you want, look at your skills. What can you do? How can you learn to do more? How can you get ready for the jobs that will be around tomorrow? School is one place to pick up special job skills. In some high school classes, you can learn such office skills as running a computer. In some, you can learn to work with wood and metal or to fix cars. Some people pick up skills by learning on the job. But, of course, you have to get a job before you can pick up skills in this way. It will have to be a job that doesn't take a special skill. You might get a job helping someone who works with electricity. Then you can watch and learn from this person.

You already know one way to find a job in the real world: look in the want ads. But there are other ways, too. You might look through the yellow pages. What catches your eye? Call around to businesses that interest you. Ask if they need help. You might walk around and look for **Help Wanted** signs. Many people find jobs through family or friends. Is your uncle's company looking for someone? Do your friends who have jobs know of anything that might open up where they work? There is only one way to find out. Ask around.

Once you know of a job you want to go for, you have to put your best foot forward. Getting the job may well take more than filling out a form. You may have to go through some kind of interview. In an interview, you meet someone from the business and answer questions face to face. A good interview can get the job for you.

How can you do well in a job interview? Here are a few points to keep in mind.

1. Try to look right for the job. Your clothes and hair are important. If you have a chance, look around the place of work before your interview. See what other people are wearing. You should wear the same kinds of clothes.

2. Before the interview, think about the questions you may be asked. Practice your answers. You can't guess every question, of course. But some questions come up in most job interviews. Here are some of those questions.
    - Why do you want this job?
    - How far did you go in school?
    - What skills do you have?
    - Have you done work like this before? When?
    - Why did you leave your last job, if you had one?
    - Why will you be good at this job?
    - Who can we call that knows you and can tell us about your work?

3. Get to the interview on time. In fact, get there early. So what if you have to sit in the waiting room for awhile? You can use that time to calm down and catch your breath.

4. Once the interview starts, listen carefully to each question. Answer just what is asked. Look the other person in the eye as you talk.

Finding Main Ideas and Details

Jobs is all about how to get a job in the real world. It looks at four main ideas that have to do with getting a job. These main ideas are listed as headings below. Write a detail on each line under the four headings. Use the choices in the box.

Call around, walk around, and ask around.
Take classes in school.
Look in the want ads.
Look right for the job.
Be on time.
Pick a job that goes with who you are and what you like.
Learn on the job.
Practice your answers.
Be friendly.

1. How to pick the kind of work that would be best for you

_____

2. How to get the skills you will need for the jobs of tomorrow

_____

_____

3. How to find out about jobs that may be open

_____

_____

4. How to do well in a job interview

_____

_____

_____

_____

12. DANA GETS A JOB

Dana looks at the number on the building. Yes, this is the place. She's scared, but she needs the job. She hopes she will do OK in this interview.

She goes through the front doors and finds herself in a big office. A young man is sitting there with his head down, working on something. "Hi," she says to him. "I called you yesterday about the ad in the paper—about the job. I was told to come in at 10:00 today. I hope I'm not late."

The young man looks up. Then he jumps to his feet. Dana says, "Oh!" She knows him. "Aren't you—" But she forgets his name. "You were at the used car place."

"Yes, I was. Good to see you again, Kate."

"Dana," she says.

His face gets all red. "Right, Dana. What brings you here?"

"As I said, I'm interested in the job."

"You are? I mean, you are! Right. Let me just look in the book. Oh, yes. Here you are. I don't know anything about it. Let me see if Mr. Henson is ready for you." The young man backs away, turns, and goes through a door. A few minutes later, he comes back out. "Go ahead," he says.

Dana goes into the office where Mr. Henson is waiting. He is a big man. He looks at her. "I'm Mr. Henson. Please sit down," he says. "Now, tell me about yourself. Do you know how to use a computer?"

"No. Is that important?"

"Important? I should say so. You are good with numbers, aren't you?"

"Not really," says Dana. "Numbers and I just don't get along—"

"Is that so? Well, did you ever keep books before?"

"No, I can't say that I did. But—"

"No? Young woman, you did not read our ad very carefully. This is a fast-moving business. A lot of bills come in and go out. A lot of money goes through this building. We must have someone who already knows how to do this kind of work. We don't have time for someone who has to learn on the job. Now, Dan will show you to—"

"But Mr. Henson, the ad I saw said something about running machines."

"Oh, that job." A long moment goes by. At last, Mr. Henson says, "But you're a woman."

"Yes, but the ad didn't say the job was only for men."

"Well, no, but do you understand what the job is? We put up houses and other buildings. We have a lot of trucks and power tools and other machines. So we run our own shop to fix things that break. That's where we need someone. Why do you think you could do that kind of work?"

Just then, Dan's uncle comes into the room. He says, "May I talk to you for a moment, Henson?"

The two men go to a corner of the room and talk for awhile. Mr. Henson comes back. "I understand you know one of my workers. You helped him buy a car."

"No," says Dana, "I helped him **not** to buy a car. I let him know the car he was about to buy was no good."

"How could you tell?"

Dana tells Mr. Henson how she could tell the car had a bad engine. Then she tells him how she comes to know so much about machines.

Mr. Henson listens and looks interested. "Well," he says at last, "I'll tell you what. We have a truck with a bad engine in the shop right now. You come in tomorrow. Show me what you can do with it. If you can prove to me that you know your way around machines, you've got the job. It would be a first for us—a woman working in our machine shop. But if you can do the work—hey, why not, I guess."

Dana has a sunny face when she walks out of Mr. Henson's office. Dan meets her at the front door. "How did it go in there?" he asks.

"Not bad," she says. "I have a feeling you put in a good word for me. Am I right?"

"I just told my uncle what happened the other day at that used car place. He said he thought it would be of interest to Mr. Henson."

"You never called me," says Dana. "I guess you didn't need my help after all. Did you buy a car already?"

"No. In fact, I'm going out to look at one tonight. Would you like to go with me? It will put you to a lot of trouble, but I'll make it up to you. I'll buy you dinner."

"OK," says Dana. She walks out of the building then and stands there for awhile looking at the city. She feels as if her new life is really taking off at last. Inside the building, Dan is feeling just the same way.

Writing a Summary

The sentences below tell about events in **Dana Gets a Job**. Use seven of these sentences to write a summary of the story. Remember that a summary gives only the most important events. It leaves out details.

Dana comes to Henson Homes to interview for a job.
Dana looks at the number on the building.
Mr. Henson thinks she wants a job keeping books.
Dana tells him she wants the job in the machine shop.
Mr. Henson asks why she thinks she can do that job.
Dan's uncle talks to Mr. Henson about Dana.
Mr. Henson listens and looks interested.
Mr. Henson makes up his mind to let Dana try the job.
On her way out, Dana runs into Dan.
Dana finds out that Dan put in a good word for her.
Dan asks Dana out, and she says yes.

_____

_____

_____

_____

_____

_____

_____

_____

_____

_____

Getting to Know Characters

You know that characters are the people in a story. The way some characters look, talk, feel, and what they do changes over time. Other characters do not change.

You have read all about Dana and Dan. By the end of this book, are these characters the same or different from the way they were at the start? Use your own words to complete the sentences.

1. At first, Dana seems scared to be in the city. By the end of the story, she

_____

_____

_____

_____

2. At first, Dan does not do anything with his life. At the end of the story, he

_____

_____

_____

_____

3. At first, Mr. Henson does not want to give Dana a job. At the end of the story, he

_____

_____

_____

_____

Who's Changed?

Did all the characters change?

Who did not change? Write their names. _____

_____

Who did change? Write their names. _____

_____

What Do You Think?

Get together with one or more friends who have read this story. Talk about the new job Dana will be starting. Do you think this is a good job for her? Will she do well at it? Why or why not?

Think About Tomorrow

Where will you be in five years? Write a letter to yourself. Write down what kind of job you will have. Will you keep going to school? Where will you be living?

When you are done writing this letter to yourself, save it. You may want to open it in five years and see if your dreams came true.

Dear _____,

_____

_____

_____

_____

_____

_____

_____

_____

                                        _____

                                        _____

_____ ❧ _____

PRACTICE LESSONS

LESSON 7.1

A. Write the correct words on the lines to complete each sentence.

1. | business   information   form |

   Dana filled out the job _____ that asked for all kinds
   of _____.

2. | page   pages   paragraphs |

   I wrote some _____ in class today, and they filled over
   three _____.

3. | important   clothes   listed |

   I _____ the two places where my mom works under the
   "_____ information" part of the form.

4. | movie   movies   newspaper |

   Will looked in the _____ to see what _____ were
   showing this week.

5. | yesterday   movie   basketball   events |

   Jared and I went to the _____ game _____.

6. | score   sport   baskets   piece |

   Did Mike get any _____, and what was the _____ of
   the game?

7. | take   office   fill   form |

   Be sure to be careful as you _____ out this job _____.

8. | bench   floor   basket   player |

   The coach kept him on the _____ because he couldn't seem to
   make a _____.

B. Write a sentence using the words above the sentence lines.

1. article   paragraph

_____

_____

2. sports   teams

_____

_____

3. less   brings

_____

_____

C. Find a word in the box that will complete each sentence below. Use each word once. You will not use all of the words in the box.

basketball	breaks	business
cans	clothes	events
fun	brings	less

1. If you are having a good time, you are having _____.

2. The things we wear are called _____.

3. If something is not more, it is _____.

4. If something comes apart, we say that it _____.

5. If your dad owns a shop, we would say he is in _____.

D. Read *The Parts of a Newspaper* on page 10 again. Write three questions you could answer by looking in a newspaper.

_____

_____

_____

A. Write the correct words on the lines to complete each sentence.

1. | state   grouped   events |

   I think there will be some _____ that will go along with the
   _____ basketball championship games.

2. | business   tool   businesses |

   When I need a new _____ to fix my car, I know there are at least
   three _____ where I can buy it.

3. | clothes   bring   shopping |

   Dana will need to _____ a lot of money with her to buy all the
   _____ she wants.

4. | shops   sport   buys |

   Bill _____ things for every _____ he likes—baseball,
   basketball, and running.

5. | told   sports   baseball   grouped |

   Yesterday Mr. Winter _____ us so that each group could play
   different _____ in PE class.

6. | sign   shut   shuts   signs |

   At the end of the day, Mrs. Weeks _____ down the shop and
   puts a "Closed" _____ on the door.

7. | shopping   skills   interesting   list |

   When Carmen and I went _____, we found a lot of
   _____ things to buy.

8. | interested   articles   interest   times |

   I read three _____ in the newspaper today that would
   _____ you.

B. Write a sentence using the words above the sentence lines.

1. skills   yesterday

   _____

   _____

2. bench   basketball

   _____

   _____

3. important   clock

   _____

   _____

C. Find a word in the box that will complete each sentence below. Use each word once. You will not use all of the words in the box.

list	movie	name	piece
sign	skill	state	

1. If you are good at something, you have a _____.

2. If you want a small part of something, you could say that you want a
   _____ of it.

3. When you write down things you want to remember to buy, you
   make a _____.

4. If you look at ads on the freeway, you are likely looking at a _____.

5. If you live in California, you would say that California is the _____
   in which you live.

D. Read *Dana on Her Own* on pages 12–13 again. Summarize the story in your own words.

   _____

   _____

   _____

A. Write the correct words on the lines to complete each sentence.

1. | quickly   add   information |

   If you can _____ up our part of the bill _____, we can
   pay and then leave the restaurant.

2. | darker   power   electric |

   The _____ went out all over town, so our street is
   _____ tonight than on most other nights.

3. | aunt   uncle   business |

   He lives with his _____ and _____.

4. | playground   writing   special |

   There are some _____ events taking place Saturday at
   the _____.

5. | engine   loud   model |

   That _____ has a special _____ in it that most cars
   don't have.

6. | blocks   block   black   engine |

   Bill's new _____ car is parked three _____ from here.

7. | rooms   schools   workers   dream |

   Mr. Stormer and his family built their _____ house with 11
   _____ in it.

8. | letting   block   writing   town |

   I am _____ my sister play at the park down the _____.

B. Write a sentence using the words above the sentence lines.

1. quick   loud

_____

_____

2. example   special

_____

_____

3. power   number

_____

_____

C. Find a word in the box that will complete each sentence below. Use each word once. You will not use all of the words in the box.

playground	darker	aunt
quickly	number	piece
skill	small	state

1. A place for kids to play could be called a _____.

2. You can make the picture on your TV lighter or _____.

3. Your mom's sister is your _____.

4. When you do something fast, you do it _____.

5. Every telephone has a telephone _____.

D. Read _Shopping the Want Ads_ on pages 18–19 again. Write a want ad for your dream job. Be sure to include the type of job, duties, salary, and contact person. You can use the sample ad on page 19 as an example.

_____

_____

_____

LESSON 7.4

A. Write the correct words on the lines to complete each sentence.

1. | quick   power   rooms |

   "Clean your _____—and make it _____," Mom says to my sister and me.

2. | schools   aunt   blocks |

   Since I started living with my _____, I've gone to three different _____.

3. | black   using   letting |

   Dana is _____ me wear her _____ jeans to the basketball game.

4. | dream   blocks   block |

   Is your house one _____ from the school or two _____ from the school?

5. | dream   model   rooms   number |

   There is a special _____ _____ on your TV set.

6. | life   power   dream   water |

   My _____ is to have a car that has a lot of _____.

7. | playground   slows   side   looks |

   If he _____ down as he goes by the _____, we can see his new truck better.

8. | wouldn't   quickly   engine   yesterday |

   The man is going to work on my car's _____ _____, so I won't have to wait too long.

B. Write a sentence using the words above the sentence lines.

1. letting   block

_____

_____

2. black   model

_____

_____

3. quickly   uncle

_____

_____

C. Find a word in the box that will complete each sentence below. Use each word once. You will not use all of the words in the box.

blocks	dream	engine	example
loud	power	rooms	slows

1. When something makes a lot of noise, we say it is _____.

2. Another word for _hope_ is _____.

3. A car or truck has an _____ to make it run.

4. If something doesn't go as fast as it used to, it _____ down.

5. _____ are something a kid might play with.

D. Read _New in the City_ on pages 21–23 again. Think about yourself and your best friend. Write two sentences explaining how the two of you are alike and two sentences explaining how you are different.

_____

_____

_____

A. Write the correct words on the lines to complete each sentence.

1. | minutes   hour   example |

   An _____ is made up of 60 _____.

2. | burn   brother   burned |

   My _____ cooked dinner last night, but he
   _____ everything.

3. | special   supposed   boy's |

   The little _____ dog was _____ to follow him
   home, but somehow the dog got lost.

4. | miss   suppose   missing |

   Do you _____ we could look for my _____ book
   before we go to school?

5. | below   above   steps |

   He went up the _____ so he would be _____ the
   baseball field.

6. | store   school   hang   hangs |

   Jake _____ around the jeans _____ for hours just
   trying to make up his mind about what to buy.

7. | too   minutes   hours   hour |

   That movie is two _____ and three _____ long.

8. | uncle's   aunt   tools   younger |

   Dad used my _____ _____ to fix his car.

B. Write a sentence using the words above the sentence lines.

1. kid's   step

   _____

   _____

2. mark   brother

   _____

   _____

3. easy   hangs

   _____

   _____

C. Find a word in the box that will complete each sentence below. Use each word once. You will not use all of the words in the box.

once	pieces	pulling	second
seconds	suppose	taking	younger

1. If you are not pushing something, you might be _____ it.

2. If your brother is not as old as you, then he is _____.

3. If you break a glass, it is likely in many _____.

4. When you want to do something only one time, we say you
   do it _____.

5. After first base, you run to _____ base.

D. Read *Reading Directions* on pages 28–29 again. Write a short paragraph explaining what might happen if you didn't read and follow directions carefully.

   _____

   _____

   _____

A. Write the correct words on the lines to complete each sentence.

1. | list   pieces   missing |

   I am _____ the three most important _____ of paper.

2. | steps   floor   kid's |

   That little _____ ball fell down the _____.

3. | minute   supposed   time |

   We're _____ to be there by now, so we don't have a

   _____ to lose.

4. | tools   above   steps |

   Just put the _____ down on the _____ when you're

   through with them.

5. | missing   boy's   brother   step |

   The _____ little _____ went with him to the playground.

6. | burned   lost   once   above |

   _____ she told me that she had _____ dinner, I didn't

   want to eat.

7. | uncle   younger   above   steps |

   My _____ brother was standing _____ me on the stairs.

8. | minute   hour   uncle's   mark |

   My _____ truck can hold the table, and it won't take more than

   an _____ to get it moved.

B. Write a sentence using the words above the sentence lines.

1. above   boy's

_____

_____

2. foods   burned

_____

_____

3. hour   tools

_____

_____

C. Find a word in the box that will complete each sentence below. Use each word once. You will not use all of the words in the box.

hours	table	brother	store
easy	light	minutes	sister

1. There are 60 _____ in an hour.

2. When you eat dinner, you most likely will sit at a _____.

3. Your uncle is your dad's _____.

4. A place to shop is a _____.

5. If something is not hard, we say it is _____.

D. Read _Dan Takes the Bus_ on pages 32–33 again. Summarize the story in your own words.

_____

_____

_____

A. Write the correct words on the lines to complete each sentence.

1. | closely   close   doctor |

   The _____ looked at Carmen's arm _____ to make sure there was no sign of a break.

2. | correct   correctly   person |

   Not one _____ in our history class answered all the test questions _____.

3. | company   sound   buzzer |

   The _____ sounded at the front door, and I knew our _____ was here for dinner.

4. | empty   correct   carefully   trick |

   Read the form _____ and make sure you fill it in with the _____ information.

5. | persons   numbers   papers   correct |

   I can't understand these _____ you gave me because they're just filled with _____.

6. | empty   security   ball   along |

   That building is pretty much _____, but it still has a _____ team that works there.

7. | filling   breaking   wrong   trick |

   Mike is showing us a _____ glass that is _____ itself with water.

8. | leaves   growing   stays   hitting |

   If Carmen _____ in that house, she's going to start _____ plants outdoors.

B. Write a sentence using the words above the sentence lines.

1. company   closely

_____

_____

2. trick   stays

_____

_____

3. buzzer   security

_____

_____

C. Find a word in the box that will complete each sentence below. Use each word once. You will not use all of the words in the box.

persons	months	parents	ago
empty	brothers	days	when

1. Another way to say _people_ is _____.

2. There are 12 _____ in a year.

3. Your mom and dad are your _____.

4. A word that means _in times past_ is _____.

5. If something is not full, it can be called _____.

D. Read _Filling Out Forms_ on pages 37–38 again. Write down three times when you might need to fill out a form.

_____

_____

_____

LESSON 7.8

A. Write the correct words on the lines below to complete each sentence.

1. | growing   carefully   filling |

   I am _____ my can so I can water the _____ plants.

2. | company   ago   month |

   Last _____, Mr. Wills' _____ moved to a new office building.

3. | parents   correct   correctly |

   Mrs. Woods told us to fill out the form _____ and have one of our _____ sign it.

4. | correctly   correct   numbers   trick |

   If I add in all these _____, my bank book will be _____.

5. | buzzer   brothers   papers   mom |

   One of my _____ answered the front door _____.

6. | trick   empty   closely   yellow |

   Watch _____ and I will show you a _____.

7. | yesterday   ago   paper   papers |

   I saw those _____ a long time _____, but I haven't seen them since.

8. | stays   pictures   person   persons |

   My aunt is a _____ who _____ inside all the time.

B. Write a sentence using the words above the sentence lines.

1. filling   carefully

   _____

   _____

2. empty   persons

   _____

   _____

3. numbers   month

   _____

   _____

C. Find a word in the box that will complete each sentence below. Use each word once. You will not use all of the words in the box.

buzzer	company	correct	doctor
growing	month	stays	trick

1. If someone is coming to your house, you could say
   you're having _____.

2. A person who takes care of sick people is a _____.

3. If a plant is getting bigger, you could say it is _____.

4. If an answer is wrong, you might say it is not _____.

5. If your dog can sit up, it knows a _____.

D. Read *A Great Apartment* on pages 40–41 again. Write an advertisement for your home. Be sure to include the number of rooms, special features, and anything else that would make a person want to live there.

_____

_____

_____

A. Write the correct words on the lines to complete each sentence.

1. | guard   he'll   they've |

   _____ have to ask the security _____ to let him in the building.

2. | clap   crowd   clapping |

   The _____ was _____ for the championship team.

3. | themselves   himself   spider's |

   If they look closely, they can see the _____ web

   for _____.

4. | scores   slams   shoot |

   The basketball player _____ the ball into the basket

   and _____.

5. | scores   seconds   shoot |

   There were only _____ left in the game, and the player had

   to _____.

6. | rule   court   faces   clap |

   The crowd started to _____ as the team came out on the

   basketball _____.

7. | looks   faces   shoot   shoots |

   Robin _____ the basket and _____ the ball.

8. | jeans   price   pair   money |

   That is too high a _____ for a _____ of pants.

B. Write a sentence using the words above the sentence lines.

1. shooting   slam

_____

_____

2. understanding   streets

_____

_____

3. jumps   rule

_____

_____

C. Find a word in the box that will complete each sentence below. Use each word once. You will not use all of the words in the box.

guarding	trick	passed	sunglasses
growing	month	seconds	trick

1. If someone is watching you, you could say he or she is

_____ you.

2. If your dog can play dead, you could say he knows a _____.

3. If a friend walks by you, you could say she _____ by.

4. Something you wear in the sun is a pair of _____.

5. There are 60 of these in a minute: _____.

D. Read _Understanding Ads_ on pages 46–49 again. Write a short paragraph about a time when something looked good in an advertisement, but when you bought it, it wasn't that good after all.

_____

_____

_____

A. Write the correct words on the lines to complete each sentence.

1. | rules   slam   understanding |

   I'm having a hard time _____ the _____ of the game.

2. | guarding   tricks   shots |

   One of his best _____ is _____ two players at one time.

3. | buildings   passes   streets |

   On the city _____, a car _____ by every two seconds.

4. | jump   low   slam |

   If you _____ the door too hard, it will make the dog _____.

5. | Mike   shelter   court   he'll |

   _____ have to learn to live with our nation's laws or he will end up in _____.

6. | jumps   shooting   shot   passed |

   Dan _____ the ball to Jared, who was good at _____ baskets from the middle of the basketball court.

7. | crowd   jeans   sunglasses   slam |

   If you wear _____, you can see the _____ at the baseball field much better.

8. | eyes   faces   clap   clapping |

   All the people had smiles on their _____ as they were _____ for the team.

B. Write a sentence using the words above the sentence lines.

1. faces   court

  _____

  _____

2. passes   crowd

  _____

  _____

3. themselves rules

  _____

  _____

C. Find a word in the box that will complete each sentence below. Use each word once. You will not use all of the words in the box.

| clap | he'll | he's | moment |
| money | open | price | slam |

1. When you shut the door hard, you _____ it.

2. If you want to know how much you will pay for something, you want to know the _____ .

3. A short time could be called a _____.

4. A shorter way of saying "he will" is _____.

5. If people like a show or a game, they will _____.

D. Read *A Good Used Car* on pages 51–52 again. Summarize the story in your own words.

  _____

  _____

  _____

A. Write the correct words on the lines to complete each sentence.

1. | shoot   interview   tomorrow |

   Jen is going to _____ Mr. White _____ for the
   school newspaper.

2. | sees   crowds   loves |

   He _____ being with a lot of people in big _____.

3. | listening   haven't   practice |

   _____ you been to basketball _____ yet?

4. | calm   catch   breath |

   Dana tried to _____ her _____ after running so far.

5. | chance   finds   catches |

   If she _____ a cold, there is a _____ she will not be
   playing in the championship basketball game.

6. | drive   minds   drivers   hair |

   If they don't change their _____, there will be enough
   _____ to take us all to the game in Mountain City.

7. | forward   violence   young   calm |

   I am trying to stay _____ and walk _____ slowly.

8. | chances   foster   finding   learning |

   Mike is slowly _____ to live with his _____ family.

B. Write a sentence using the words above the sentence lines.

1. chances   choices

_____

_____

2. loses   breath

_____

_____

3. calm   listens

_____

_____

C. Find a word in the box that will complete each sentence below. Use each word once. You will not use all of the words in the box.

choice	face	hair	hasn't
haven't	hurts	tomorrow	yesterday

1. If you break your arm, it _____.

2. Your _____ is on the top of your head.

3. If you can have either one thing or another thing, you

    have a _____.

4. A shorter way of saying *have not* is _____.

5. The day after today is _____.

D. Read *Jobs* on pages 56–58 again. Think about a job you would like to have someday. Write three things that you will need to do or learn about in order to be qualified for that job.

_____

_____

_____

A. Write the correct words on the lines to complete each sentence.

1. | tries   hurts   listens |

   The cop _____ to Mu Lan as she describes the car crash, and
   then he asks her if she _____ anywhere.

2. | forgets   hair   loses |

   If my dad _____ any more of his _____, he won't have
   any left at all.

3. | choice   forget   forgets |

   If Jake _____ to bring his paper to class one more time,
   Mrs. Woods will have no _____ but to give him an F.

4. | listens   sees   interviews |

   When the newsman on TV _____ someone, it seems that he
   really _____ to that person.

5. | loses   mind   calm   wrong |

   Mom seems so _____, you would think she doesn't
   _____ all the noise going on around her.

6. | now   practice   tomorrow   yesterday |

   Right now I need to _____ my guitar, but I'll go with
   you _____.

7. | foster   chances   center   crowds |

   They think my _____ of finding a _____ mom and dad
   are good.

8. | drivers   loves   chance   working |

   You didn't even give her a _____ to tell you how much she
   _____ you.

B. Write a sentence using the words above the sentence lines.

1. catch   minds

   _____

   _____

2. choice   loves

   _____

   _____

3. crowds   listens

   _____

   _____

C. Find a word in the box that will complete each sentence below. Use each word once. You will not use all of the words in the box.

breath	center	foot	forward
money	practice	wash	web

1. On the end of your leg is your _____.

2. If you run too hard, you will be out of _____.

3. If you want to get better at something, you will have to _____ it.

4. If you're not driving backward, you're driving _____.

5. If you are in the middle, you are in the _____.

D. Read *Dana Gets a Job* on pages 60–62 again. Do you think Dana will like her new job? Do you think she will be good at it? Write a short paragraph explaining your thoughts on Dana's new job.

   _____

   _____

   _____

RESPONSE TO READING

You can use these pages to record your responses to stories in the Worktext, Midway Novel, Final Novel, or anything else you may read on your own.

Title: _____

_____

_____

_____

_____

_____

_____

_____

_____

_____

_____

_____

_____

_____

_____

_____

_____

_____

_____

_____

_____

_____

Title: _____

MEMORY CHIPS

Remember to keep working with your Memory Chips. They will help you to really remember these words. Keep your Memory Chips in two groups. One group you are working with every day. The other group of Chips are words you know very well. Get out the second group about once a week. Go over them just to make sure. Keep up the good work. You have come a long way.

There are too many **ads** on TV.	IA	A **newspaper** is full of news.	IA	You need a **tool** to open a can.	IA
The work is **almost** done.	IA	A **paragraph** has one main idea.	IA	Ice **forms** on windows in winter.	IA
Read this **article** about animals.	IA	The article is three **paragraphs** long.	IA	I have some **important** news.	IA
Jen writes **articles** about outer space.	IA	Let me give you a **piece** of fish.	IA	This book has **information** about American history.	IA
Dana is a girl I know.	IA	We spent hours **shopping** for food.	IA	Let's write up a **list** of names.	IA
Did you **fill** the car with gas?	IA	The **sign** says you can't turn left here.	IA	We can learn many **skills** in school.	IA
Let's **form** a band.	IA	Mike **signs** his name on the paper.	IA	Baseball is a **sport** that many Americans like.	IA
Take the food home in a **basket**.	1A	Playing basketball takes **skill**.	IA	Americans like to watch **sports** on TV.	IA
Dana played **basketball** in high school.	1A	The dish **breaks** as it hits the floor.	1A	Carmen is in the oil **business**.	1A
Donna **brings** her dog to school one day.	1A	May I **bring** you something to drink?	1A	Well–run **businesses** often make money.	1A
Sit on the **bench**.	1A	Jake has two **baskets** full of food.	1A	Mike **buys** a newspaper every day.	1A

tool	*I*B	newspaper	*I*B	ads	*I*B
forms	*I*B	paragraph	*I*B	almost	*I*B
important	*I*B	paragraphs	*I*B	article	*I*B
information	*I*B	piece	*I*B	articles	*I*B
list	*I*B	shopping	*I*B	Dana	*I*B
skills	*I*B	sign	*I*B	fill	*I*B
sport	*I*B	signs	*I*B	form	*I*B
sports	*I*B	skill	*I*B	basket	1B
business	1B	breaks	1B	basketball	1B
businesses	1B	bring	1B	brings	1B
buys	1B	baskets	1B	bench	1B

A **clock** shows what time it is.	1A	It takes a lot of money to make **movies.**	1A	Dan's story holds Carmen's **interest.**	1A
Light **clothes** are best for summer.	1A	Most **newspapers** have sports news.	1A	It's an **interesting** story.	1A
The story was about an **event** from history.	1A	Look it up in the yellow **pages.**	1A	The red box has **less** food in it than the green one.	1A
The news is full of exciting **events** today.	1A	Our team won by a **score** of 100–98.	1A	Jake **listed** the last ten books he had read.	1A
Playing games is **fun.**	1A	Tom **shuts** the door.	1A	The **movie** is about an outlaw.	1A
The big pictures were **grouped** together.	1A	I like open **spaces.**	1A	Both **teams** played hard.	1A
Bill's aunt is named Jean.	3A	California is a **state.**	1A	Where was she **yesterday**?	1A
Mike has **black** hair.	3A	I had a bad **dream** last night.	3A	Follow my **example.**	3A
Get a **block** of ice from the freezer.	3A	Jen put a new **engine** in her car.	3A	The car in the story is a **Stormer.**	3A
The truck **blocks** the whole street.	3A	Bill will **add** a player to his team.	3A	I'm **letting** this small fish go.	3A
It was **darker** after the sun went down.	3A	My mom's sister is my **aunt.**	3A	Don't talk in such a **loud** voice!	3A

interest	1B	movies	1B	clock	1B
interesting	1B	newspapers	1B	clothes	1B
less	1B	pages	1B	event	1B
listed	1B	score	1B	events	1B
movie	1B	shuts	1B	fun	1B
teams	1B	spaces	1B	grouped	1B
yesterday	1B	state	1B	Bill's	3B
example	3B	dream	3B	black	3B
Stormer	3B	engine	3B	block	3B
letting	3B	add	3B	blocks	3B
loud	3B	aunt	3B	darker	3B

Luis likes to build **model** ships.	3A	The workers have **power** tools.	3A	The **schools** need more money.	3A
What is your telephone **number**?	3A	Take a **quick** look at this letter.	3A	The car **slows** down for the light.	3A
The kids are playing on the **playground**.	3A	Ana runs **quickly** down the street.	3A	What's so **special** about today?	3A
The stars are **above** us.	5A	This house has five **rooms**.	3A	My **uncle** came to see us.	3A
That is a **boy's** bike.	5A	Take it **easy**.	5A	All the **pieces** are falling into place at last.	5A
Luis is my **brother**.	5A	Some **foods** are hot.	5A	I'm **pulling** for Tom to win the race.	5A
The house **burned** down in the big fire.	5A	The cloth **hangs** on the line.	5A	Tom comes in **second**.	5A
This will only take a **minute**.	5A	An **hour** can feel like a long time.	5A	**Step** into the ring.	5A
Inez can run a mile in five **minutes**.	5A	There are 24 **hours** in a day.	5A	Take two **steps** south.	5A
The money is **missing**!	5A	The **kid's** smile makes people feel good.	5A	Jen runs a computer **store**.	5A
I only saw that man **once**.	5A	Do not **mark** up the wall.	5A	Do you **suppose** dogs can think?	5A

schools	3B	power	3B	model	3B
slows	3B	quick	3B	number	3B
special	3B	quickly	3B	playground	3B
uncle	3B	rooms	3B	above	5B
pieces	5B	easy	5B	boy's	5B
pulling	5B	foods	5B	brother	5B
second	5B	hangs	5B	burned	5B
step	5B	hour	5B	minute	5B
steps	5B	hours	5B	minutes	5B
store	5B	kid's	5B	missing	5B
suppose	5B	mark	5B	once	5B

Inez is **supposed** to be the boss.	5A	**There's** no need to be sad.	5A	My **uncle's** brother is my dad.	5A
Dinner is on the **table**.	5A	Get the right **tools** or the job.	5A	My dad is **younger** than my uncle.	5A
Tom works for an oil **company**.	7A	Answer the questions **correctly**.	7A	The **security** guard saw the thief.	7A
You get one point for each **correct** answer.	7A	Ask a **doctor** why you are sick.	7A	Wilma **stays** home a lot these days.	7A
A **person** can say whatever he or she thinks.	7A	The box is **empty**.	7A	Look out—it's a **trick**!	7A
Two **persons** came to the meeting late.	7A	Keep **filling** my dish with that good food.	7A	Pick that dish up **carefully**.	7A
Luis was born 18 years **ago**.	7A	A **growing** boy needs lots of food.	7A	My name was in the **papers**.	7A
Luis and César are **brothers**.	7A	A **month** is four weeks long.	7A	My **parents** are getting old now.	7A
The game ends when the **buzzer** goes off.	7A	Jen writes down two telephone **numbers**.	7A	Don't follow the car ahead of you too **closely**.	7A
Clap your hands.	9A	People were **clapping** for the hero.	9A	Take some **chances**.	7A
There was a big **crowd** at the game.	9A	A basketball **court** is not a court of law.	9A	The **guard** caught the thief.	9A

uncle's	5B	there's	5B	supposed	5B
younger	5B	tools	5B	table	5B
security	7B	correctly	7B	company	7B
stays	7B	doctor	7B	correct	7B
trick	7B	empty	7B	person	7B
carefully	7B	filling	7B	persons	7B
papers	7B	growing	7B	ago	7B
parents	7B	month	7B	brothers	7B
closely	7B	numbers	7B	buzzer	7B
chances	7B	clapping	9B	clap	9B
guard	9B	court	9B	crowd	9B

The dog is **guarding** the bone.	9A	What are the **rules** of this game?	9A	Wear **sunglasses** to keep out the light.	9A
Tom thinks **he'll** be home soon.	9A	Tom **scores** about 30 points a game.	9A	Tom and Ana keep to **themselves**.	9A
How high can you **jump**?	9A	The game will be over in a few **seconds**.	9A	Don't try to play any **tricks** now.	9A
The boy **jumps** over the wall.	9A	They will **shoot** a movie on my street.	9A	I have a hard time **understanding** you.	9A
The sound is so **low** that he can hardly hear it.	9A	They will be **shooting** that movie very soon.	9A	Jared **wears** a red hat.	9A
I'll be with you in just a **moment**.	9A	He **shoots** the gun but misses.	9A	**Weren't** you at the movies on Saturday?	9A
What a **pair** those two make!	9A	The doctor will give you a **shot**.	9A	This is mine, and that is **yours**.	9A
Mu Lan **passed** the science test.	9A	Don't **slam** the door.	9A	The **price** is high.	9A
The bus **passes** me every day as I walk to school.	9A	Robert always **slams** the door on his way out.	9A	Is there a **rule** against writing on walls?	9A
The building **faces** north.	9A	A **spider's** web is its home.	9A	The city has big **streets** with lots of cars	9A
Don't get excited —stay **calm**.	11A	Can you **catch** the ball?	11A	Dana **catches** the ball.	11A

sunglasses	9B	rules	9B	guarding	9B
themselves	9B	scores	9B	he'll	9B
tricks	9B	seconds	9B	jump	9B
understanding	9B	shoot	9B	jumps	9B
wears	9B	shooting	9B	low	9B
weren't	9B	shoots	9B	moment	9B
yours	9B	shot	9B	pair	9B
price	9B	slam	9B	passed	9B
rule	9B	slams	9B	passes	9B
streets	9B	spider's	9B	faces	9B
catches	11B	catch	11B	calm	11B

The building is in the **center** of the city 11A	Inez will let her **hair** grow long. 11A	It takes **practice** to get good at anything. 11A
There is a **chance** of snow tomorrow. 11A	**I haven't** seen Inez today. 11A	Don't put off till **tomorrow** what you can do today. 11A
Miles takes too many **chances** in his car. 11A	My foot still **hurts**. 11A	Dan often **forgets** where he has put things. 11A
When you vote, you make a **choice**. 11A	An **interview** is a face to face meeting. 11A	Take one step **forward**. 11A
Tom faces some hard **choices** in his life 11A	Wilma **interviews** Jake for the job. 11A	The boy lives in a **foster** home. 11A
The show is getting big **crowds**. 11A	I'm **learning** a lot about science in my new job. 11A	Ana **loves** to help people who are in trouble. 11A
Bus **drivers** have a hard job. 11A	A good boss **listens** to the workers. 11A	Ana is sad when she **loses** a game. 11A
Can we get to the store on **foot**? 11A	You can learn a lot by **listening**. 11A	Kids have **minds** of their own. 11A

practice	11B	hair	11B	center	11B
tomorrow	11B	haven't	11B	chance	11B
forgets	11B	hurts	11B	chances	11B
forward	11B	interview	11B	choice	11B
foster	11B	interviews	11B	choices	11B
loves	11B	learning	11B	crowds	11B
loses	11B	listens	11B	drivers	11B
minds	11B	listening	11B	foot	11B